Don't Fix You

Introduction: Why "Don't
- The Problem with "Fixing"
- My Story
- A New Way Forward
- Why This Matters

Chapter 1: The Credit Repair Trap
- The Promise of a Quick Fix
- The Hidden Costs of Credit Repair Services
- The Cycle of Dependence
- Why Fixing Isn't Enough
  - Key Takeaway:

Chapter 2: Understanding Your Credit Story
- Your Credit Report: A Snapshot of Your Financial Journey
- Decoding Your Credit Score: The Magic Number
- The Power of Awareness
- Breaking Down the Myths
- Credit's Hidden Impact
  - Key Takeaway

Chapter 3: Don't Fix It—Rebuild It
- Fixing Isn't the Endgame
- The Power of Building First
- Why Fixing Without Building Doesn't Work
- Rebuilding Starts with Understanding
- Tools and Resources for Rebuilding
  - Key Takeaway

Chapter 4: Focus on Financial Freedom
- From Scarcity to Abundance
- The Power of Having a Why
- Breaking Free from the System
- Entrepreneurship: A Path to Freedom
- The Importance of Organization and Seeking Help
- Real-Life Success Stories
- Aligning Credit Goals with Financial Independence
  - Key Takeaway

Chapter 5: Credit Beyond the Score
- More Than Just a Number
- How Credit Impacts Daily Life
- Using Credit as a Tool, Not a Crutch
- Long-Term Habits for a Strong Financial Foundation

The Bigger Picture
   Key Takeaway

Chapter 6: Building a Legacy

The Power of Financial Literacy
Teaching the Next Generation
Breaking Generational Cycles
The Bigger Picture: Credit, Wealth, and Community Impact
Leaving a Legacy
   Key Takeaway

Conclusion: Confidence Over Quick Fixes
   Why Fixing Isn't the Answer
   Take Ownership of Your Journey
   One Small Step Today
   You've Got This
   Call-to-Action:

Final Section: Ready to Take the Next Step?
   What Is Dispute Beast?
   Why Choose Dispute Beast?
      Take the First Step Today

Introduction: Why "Don't Fix Your Credit" Is the Answer

The Problem with "Fixing"

When I started my journey to investor, I believed the only way to get ahead was to fix my credit. I thought, *If I could just erase the bad stuff, everything would fall into place.* But here's the hard truth I learned: credit isn't something you "fix." It's something you build, sustain, and take control of.

The idea of "fixing" your credit feels quick and easy, doesn't it? Services promise to handle everything for you, social media gurus sell you overpriced courses, and credit apps offer automated solutions. That works for a few. A larger percentage still finds themselves stuck—confused, frustrated, and broke—because fixing isn't the solution. Building is.

My Story

I know this struggle firsthand. There was a time when I couldn't even dream of being approved for a loan, let alone securing favorable terms. I missed out on opportunities to invest in real estate—opportunities that could have changed my life—because my credit wasn't where it needed to be.

I'll never forget the embarrassment of being denied by lenders. It wasn't just about the "no"; it was about realizing I didn't even understand what they were looking at. I felt powerless, and that lack of knowledge held me back more than anything on my credit report ever could.

But what hurt even more was watching my mom struggle to make ends meet, constantly stressed about money and never given the tools to rise above it. I saw the cycle of financial hardship, and I knew I had to break it—not just for me, but for the generations that would come after me.

A New Way Forward

This book isn't about quick fixes. It's about giving you the tools, strategies, and mindset to take control of your credit—once and for all. Whether your goal is to buy a home, lower your car insurance rates, or simply stop feeling stuck every time you think about money, this journey will empower you to make real, lasting changes.

We're going to break down the myths and misconceptions that hold you back. We'll decode credit reports and scores, so you'll finally understand how they work and what truly matters. And we'll build sustainable habits that ensure your financial future is secure—not just for you, but for the people you care about.

Why This Matters

Good credit is more than a number. It's about freedom. It's about walking into a bank with confidence, knowing you have options. It's about creating a legacy, breaking generational cycles of financial struggle, and providing opportunities for yourself and others.

You deserve to feel proud of your financial journey—not embarrassed or overwhelmed. This book will show you how to take the reins, rewrite your credit story, and unlock the life you've always wanted.

Let's get started.

CHAPTER 1: THE CREDIT REPAIR TRAP

The Promise of a Quick Fix

"We'll fix your credit in no time!" How often have you heard this promise? Late-night commercials, social media ads, and even well-meaning friends have all touted credit repair as the magical solution to financial woes. The allure is undeniable: someone else swoops in, wipes away your mistakes, and hands you a shiny new credit score. But here's the reality—they're not telling you the full story.

Quick fixes often come with high fees, temporary results, and no real education about how to maintain your credit. Worse, they can lead you back into the same habits and problems that got you into trouble in the first place. Fixing your credit without understanding it is like patching a leaky boat without addressing the hole.

DON'T FIX YOUR CREDIT

The Hidden Costs of Credit Repair Services

Credit repair services often sell convenience at a steep price. These companies may dispute negative items on your report—sometimes even legitimate ones. While this might temporarily boost your score, it doesn't address the underlying behaviors or systems that led to the issue.

Here's the kicker: credit repair companies can't do anything you can't do yourself. That's right—you have the power to challenge inaccuracies, negotiate with creditors, and improve your credit without paying someone else hundreds (or even thousands) of dollars.

The Cycle of Dependence

Relying on someone else to fix your credit creates a cycle of dependence. When you don't understand what affects your credit score or how to manage it, you'll keep returning to external services for help. This keeps you stuck, always needing a rescue, instead of taking control of your financial journey.

Breaking out of this trap requires a mindset shift. Instead of looking for someone to "fix" your credit, you need to embrace the idea of *building* it—slowly, intentionally, and sustainably. This isn't just about improving a number; it's about transforming your relationship with money and credit.

Why Fixing Isn't Enough

Think of credit repair as slapping a band-aid on a deep wound. Sure, it might look better temporarily, but without treating the root cause, the problem will resurface. True credit growth comes from understanding your financial habits, addressing errors on your report, and creating a strategy for long-term improvement.

Credit is more than just a score—it's a reflection of how you interact with money. By focusing on education, clarity, and actionable steps, you can not only improve your credit but also gain the confidence to walk into any lender's office and secure the best rates and opportunities.

Key Takeaway:

Stop looking for someone to "fix" your credit. Instead, take ownership of your financial future by learning the basics, addressing underlying habits, and building a sustainable credit profile that serves you for life.

CHAPTER 2: UNDERSTANDING YOUR CREDIT STORY

Your Credit Report: A Snapshot of Your Financial Journey

Your credit report isn't just a boring document full of numbers and jargon—it's your financial story. It tells lenders how you've managed money in the past and gives them a sense of whether they can trust you with their money in the future. But here's the problem: most people have never been taught how to read or understand their credit report. And that's where the power imbalance begins.

Your credit report is broken down into five sections:

1. **Personal Information:** This includes your name, address, and employment history. It's basic, but errors here can still cause problems.
2. **Account Information:** This lists all your loans, credit cards, and other financial accounts, showing balances and payment history.
3. **Public Records:** Hopefully, this section is empty, but if not, it might include bankruptcies or judgments.
4. **Credit Inquiries:** This shows who's been checking your credit and why.
5. **Negative Information:** Any late payments, defaults, or collections appear here.

By learning to interpret this report, you're no longer just a number in someone else's system—you're in control.

Decoding Your Credit Score: The Magic Number

If your credit report is the story, your credit score is the headline. It's a single number that summarizes your financial reliability. Here's how it's calculated:

- **Payment History (35%)**: Are you paying your bills on time?
- **Credit Utilization (30%)**: How much of your available credit are you using?
- **Length of Credit History (15%)**: How long have your accounts been active?
- **Credit Mix (10%)**: Do you have a variety of account types, like credit cards and loans?
- **New Credit (10%)**: Have you opened a lot of accounts recently?

Understanding these factors demystifies your score and helps you focus on what matters most. The truth is, you don't need to obsess over every detail—just the big contributors.

The Power of Awareness

Most people avoid checking their credit because they're scared of what they might find. I get it—facing the truth can be tough. But ignoring it doesn't make the problem go away. In fact, it can make things worse. Errors on your report can hurt your score, and if you're not paying attention, you'll never know.

Awareness is your superpower. When you know what's in your report and what affects your score, you can take targeted action to improve it. You're no longer at the mercy of lenders—you're in control of your financial future.

Breaking Down the Myths

Let's clear up some common misconceptions about credit:

1. **Myth:** Checking your credit report will hurt your score.
   - **Truth:** Pulling your own credit report is a "soft inquiry" and doesn't affect your score at all.
2. **Myth:** Closing old accounts will improve your score.
   - **Truth:** Length of credit history is important—keeping old accounts open is usually better and CLOSING good accounts can actually hurt your score.
3. **Myth:** Your income affects your credit score.
   - **Truth:** Credit scores don't consider income; they're based on how you manage credit.

These myths hold people back, but understanding the facts empowers you to make smarter decisions.

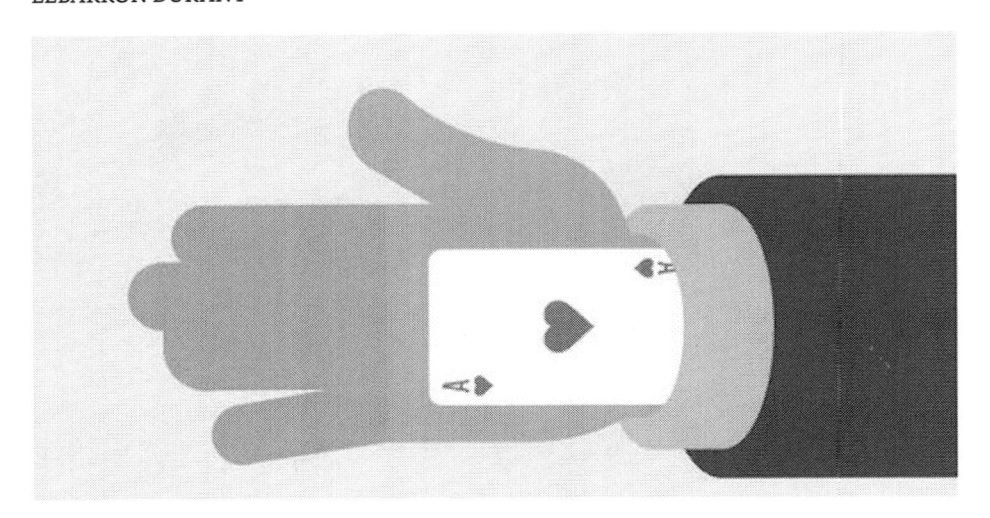

Credit's Hidden Impact

Your credit doesn't just affect your ability to get a loan—it impacts nearly every area of your financial life. Did you know your credit score can determine:

- **Your car insurance premiums?** Many insurers view credit scores as a predictor of risk.
- **Your ability to rent an apartment?** Landlords often check credit to assess reliability.
- **Your homeowners insurance rates?** A good credit score can save you money here, too.
- **Your ability to get a job?** You could miss out on a job or even lose one—especially if you need a security clearance. Poor credit makes you appear vulnerable to bribes or other risks employers want to avoid.

Credit isn't just about borrowing money—it's about creating opportunities and reducing financial stress across the board.

Key Takeaway

Understanding your credit report and score is the first step to taking control of your financial story. It's not about perfection—it's about progress. When you know what lenders are looking at, you can shift the narrative in your favor and build the financial future you deserve.

CHAPTER 3: DON'T FIX IT—REBUILD IT

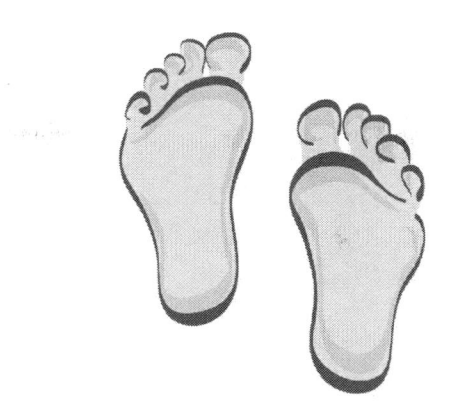

Fixing Isn't the Endgame

Let me be clear: I'm not telling you to ignore fixing your credit. Addressing negative items on your credit report and challenging inaccuracies is important, but it's not the *only* thing you need to do. Fixing your credit without understanding how credit works —or without building good habits—is like patching a leak on a sinking ship without learning how to steer.

Fixing your credit is a step, not the destination. To truly thrive financially, you need to focus first on building habits that will serve you for the long term, understanding your credit report, and learning how to use credit to your advantage.

The Power of Building First

Think of credit like building a house. Fixing negative items on your credit report is like patching cracks in the foundation—it's necessary, but it doesn't make the house livable. What truly makes your financial "house" strong and resilient is building with intention. This means:

- **Understanding Your Credit:** Know how your score is calculated, what factors matter most, and how to read your credit report like a pro.
- **Developing Good Habits:** Small, consistent actions like paying bills on time, managing credit utilization, and keeping balances low create a strong financial foundation.
- **Making Informed Choices:** Learn to use credit strategically to support your goals instead of letting it hold you back.

Once you have these fundamentals in place, fixing your credit becomes part of a broader plan—not your only plan.

Why Fixing Without Building Doesn't Work

Many people focus solely on removing negative items from their credit report, thinking it will solve everything. Here's why that approach falls short:

1. **Temporary Gains:** Fixing errors or removing old accounts might boost your score temporarily, but without good habits, you'll end up back where you started.

2. **Missed Opportunities:** If you don't understand how credit works, you might make choices—like closing old accounts—that hurt your score in the long run.

3. **Lack of Confidence:** Fixing credit without building knowledge and habits leaves you feeling uncertain and dependent on others.

Rebuilding Starts with Understanding

Here's what you should focus on first:

1. **Learn How Credit Works:**
    - Understand the key factors affecting your score: payment history, credit utilization, length of credit history, credit mix, and new credit.
    - Know what lenders look for and how to improve in these areas.
2. **Build Habits That Stick:**
    - Set up automatic payments to avoid missed deadlines.
    - Pay down high balances to reduce your credit utilization ratio.
    - Use credit responsibly—only borrow what you can repay.
3. **Fix as Part of the Process:**
    - Review your credit report for errors and dispute inaccuracies.
    - Address negative items strategically, but don't make fixing your sole focus.

Tools and Resources for Rebuilding

Rebuilding your credit doesn't have to be overwhelming. Here are tools to help you on your journey:

1. **Credit Monitoring Tools:** Track your progress and stay informed about changes to your credit score.
2. **Budgeting Apps:** Manage your finances and prioritize payments effectively.
3. **Educational Resources:** Take time to learn about credit through books, courses, or communities like the **Confident Credit Crew**.
4. **Secured Credit Cards:** Start rebuilding positive payment history if you have limited credit.

Key Takeaway

Fixing your credit is important, but it's not the only thing that matters. Focus first on understanding your credit, building strong habits, and learning how to use credit wisely. When fixing becomes part of a bigger plan, you'll not only improve your score but also gain the confidence and knowledge to maintain it for life.

You're not just fixing your credit—you're building a better financial future.

CHAPTER 4: FOCUS ON FINANCIAL FREEDOM

From Scarcity to Abundance

Your financial journey isn't just about dollars, cents, or credit scores—it's about shifting the way you think. Many of us approach credit with a scarcity mindset: *"I'll never get approved," "I'm not good with money,"* or *"It's too late for me."* These thoughts keep us stuck, focusing on what we lack instead of what's possible.

Financial freedom starts when you embrace an abundance mindset. Instead of thinking about what you don't have, focus on what you're building: a secure future, new opportunities, and a legacy that lasts beyond you.

Ask yourself: *What's my financial "why"?* Maybe it's creating a stable home for your family, starting a business, or retiring comfortably. When you know your why, it becomes easier to stay focused and committed to the journey, even when it feels challenging.

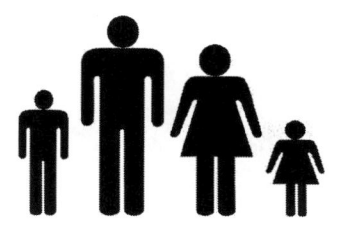

The Power of Having a Why

Think about a time when you set a goal and stayed motivated to achieve it. Chances are, there was a reason—a "why"—driving you forward. In your credit journey, having a clear and compelling reason for improving your financial health is just as important.

Your why keeps you grounded when the process feels slow or overwhelming. It reminds you that the work you're doing now isn't just about a number on a credit report; it's about creating a life of freedom and possibility.

Here's how to define your financial why:

1. Ask yourself: *What do I want my financial future to look like?*
2. Visualize it: Imagine walking into a bank, securing the loan you need, and achieving your goals.
3. Write it down: Keep it somewhere visible as a daily reminder of why you're on this journey.

Breaking Free from the System

There's a reason this information isn't widely taught. The credit and banking industries thrive on our ignorance about credit, money, and investments. They "bank" on us being uninformed about interest rates, fees, and long-term financial strategies because it keeps us dependent.

Think about it: the system capitalizes on short-term gratification—buy now, pay later. It's designed to make us consumers, not producers. It encourages us to take jobs and create problems rather than solve them. This benefits corporations and financial institutions immensely, but it keeps us in a cycle of working for money instead of making money work for us.

The good news? You have the power to break free. When you shift your mindset from scarcity to abundance, you stop playing by the rules of a system designed to keep you small. Instead, you create your own rules. There's exponential power in a mindset of solving problems, creating opportunities, and building something that lasts.

Entrepreneurship: A Path to Freedom

One of the most powerful ways to break free from the system is through entrepreneurship. When you become a producer instead of just a consumer, you open the door to financial freedom in ways you may never have imagined. Entrepreneurs not only have control over their income but also gain access to significant tax benefits, such as:

- **Deductions for Business Expenses:** Office supplies, travel, meals, and even a home office can be written off.
- **Depreciation:** Assets like vehicles, equipment, and property used for business purposes can reduce taxable income.
- **Health Insurance Deductions:** Self-employed individuals can often deduct the cost of their health insurance.

These advantages allow entrepreneurs to keep more of their earnings and reinvest in their growth.

The Importance of Organization and Seeking Help

With great opportunity comes great responsibility. To fully benefit from the advantages of entrepreneurship, you must stay organized and seek help when needed. Here's how to stay on top of things:

1. **Keep Accurate Records:** Use accounting software or hire a bookkeeper to track your expenses and income.
2. **Work with Professionals:** Consult with a tax advisor to ensure you're maximizing deductions and staying compliant with regulations.
3. **Plan Ahead:** Set aside money for taxes, emergencies, and reinvestment in your business.

Being organized isn't just about avoiding penalties—it's about creating a stable foundation that allows you to focus on growth.

Real-Life Success Stories

Sometimes, the best way to stay inspired is to hear stories of people who've been where you are—and come out stronger on the other side.

- **The Aspiring Investor:** A young professional with a low credit score and no idea where to start decided to focus on building habits instead of chasing quick fixes. By paying bills on time, disputing errors, and using a secured credit card, they went from being denied loans to securing financing for their first real estate investment within two years.
- **The Single Parent:** Struggling to make ends meet and with little credit knowledge, this individual set a goal to rebuild credit for their family's future. They started by learning to read their credit report, making small, consistent payments, and focusing on reducing utilization. Today, they're proud homeowners, providing stability for their children.
- **The Entrepreneur:** A business owner who faced rejection after rejection from lenders worked to build their credit over time. With a clear financial why—expanding their business—they created a plan, stuck with it, and eventually secured the funding needed to grow their dream.

Each of these stories has one thing in common: their why kept them moving forward.

Aligning Credit Goals with Financial Independence

Credit isn't just about approval rates or interest percentages—it's a tool to help you achieve your bigger financial goals. Here's how to align your credit journey with financial independence:

1. **Set Clear Goals:** Whether it's buying a home, starting a business, or saving for retirement, have a tangible goal to work toward.
2. **Track Your Progress:** Celebrate small wins, like paying off a credit card or seeing your score increase.
3. **Keep Your Why in Sight:** When challenges arise, remind yourself of the life you're working to create.

By aligning your credit goals with your long-term vision, you're not just building credit—you're building freedom.

Key Takeaway

Financial freedom starts with mindset, but it's sustained by action. Shift from scarcity to abundance by focusing on what's possible, not what's missing. Define your why, stay motivated by your goals, and remember: every step you take brings you closer to the life you deserve.

You're not just fixing credit—you're creating opportunities, leaving a legacy, and living with purpose.

CHAPTER 5: CREDIT BEYOND THE SCORE

More Than Just a Number

For most people, the credit score is the main focus. But your credit is so much more than that three-digit number. It touches nearly every aspect of your financial life, often in ways you don't realize.

From the interest rates you pay to the jobs you qualify for, your credit influences opportunities and costs in surprising ways. Understanding these impacts helps you see credit for what it truly is: a powerful tool when used wisely and a potential barrier when misunderstood.

How Credit Impacts Daily Life

Here are some ways your credit extends beyond the score:
1. **Car Insurance Premiums:**
    - Insurers use credit scores to predict risk. A higher score often means lower premiums, potentially saving you hundreds each year.
2. **Homeownership Opportunities:**
    - Good credit makes it easier to qualify for mortgages and secure lower interest rates, saving tens of thousands over the life of a loan.
3. **Job Prospects:**
    - Employers, especially in finance or positions requiring security clearances, often review credit as part of the hiring process. Poor credit could be a red flag, potentially costing you a job opportunity.
4. **Daily Financial Transactions:**
    - Renting an apartment, setting up utilities, or even getting a cell phone plan can involve credit checks. A strong credit profile reduces hassles and upfront deposits.

Understanding these impacts allows you to see credit as more than just a financial score—it's a tool that can make life easier and less expensive when managed well.

Using Credit as a Tool, Not a Crutch

Credit is a double-edged sword. When used wisely, it's a tool that opens doors to financial opportunities. But when relied on excessively, it becomes a crutch that leads to dependency and debt.

Here's how to use credit as a tool:

- **For Leverage, Not Lifestyle:** Use credit to invest in things that grow your financial future, like education, property, or business—not to fund unnecessary spending.
- **For Strategic Benefits:** Take advantage of credit card perks, cashback, and travel rewards, but pay balances in full each month to avoid interest.
- **For Building, Not Band-Aiding:** Use credit to build a strong profile that reflects responsibility, not as a way to cover financial gaps.

When you think of credit as a resource instead of a safety net, you empower yourself to use it intentionally and strategically.

Long-Term Habits for a Strong Financial Foundation

Maintaining good credit isn't a one-time effort—it's a lifelong practice. Here are some habits to help you sustain and strengthen your financial foundation:

1. **Monitor Regularly:**
   - Check your credit report at least once a year to catch errors, track progress, and address issues early.
2. **Stay Organized:**
   - Keep a calendar for due dates, set up autopay for bills, and regularly review your spending habits.
3. **Keep Balances Low:**
   - Aim for a credit utilization rate of under 30%. This means using less than 30% of your available credit across all accounts.
4. **Avoid Unnecessary Credit Applications:**
   - Every new application results in a hard inquiry, which can temporarily lower your score. Only apply for credit when needed.
5. **Be Patient and Consistent:**

- Building a strong credit foundation takes time. Focus on steady progress rather than quick fixes.

The Bigger Picture

Credit isn't just about loans, interest rates, or even financial convenience—it's about freedom, trust, and opportunity. When you manage your credit responsibly, you reduce financial stress and gain the flexibility to focus on what truly matters: your goals, your family, and your future.

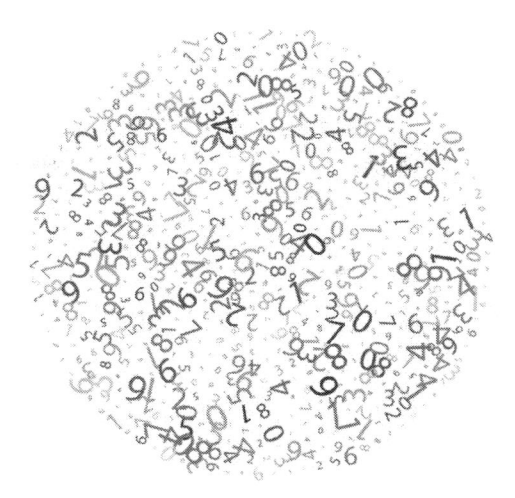

Key Takeaway

Your credit is more than just a number—it's a tool that can either simplify your life or complicate it, depending on how you use it. By understanding its broader impacts, using it strategically, and maintaining healthy financial habits, you can ensure your credit works for you, not against you.

CHAPTER 6: BUILDING A LEGACY

The Power of Financial Literacy

Imagine if you had learned about credit, saving, and financial planning as a teenager. How different would your life be today? For many of us, financial literacy wasn't part of our upbringing. Instead, we've had to navigate through trial and error, often paying a steep price for mistakes.

Now imagine being the person who changes that for the next generation. Teaching financial literacy isn't just about helping your kids understand money—it's about giving them the tools to break cycles of financial struggle and create opportunities for themselves and others.

Teaching the Next Generation

The earlier someone learns about credit and financial responsibility, the better prepared they'll be for life's opportunities and challenges. Here's how you can teach the next generation:

1. **Start with the Basics:**
    - Teach them how credit works, including the importance of on-time payments, avoiding high-interest debt, and using credit cards responsibly.
2. **Lead by Example:**
    - Show them what healthy financial habits look like. Involve them in age-appropriate discussions about budgeting, saving, and managing expenses.
3. **Use Real-Life Scenarios:**
    - Give them small opportunities to practice financial decisions, like budgeting for a school trip or managing a prepaid card.
4. **Introduce Tools Early:**
    - Use apps or games designed to teach financial literacy in an engaging way.

By normalizing conversations about credit and money, you can remove the stigma and make financial literacy a natural part of

DON'T FIX YOUR CREDIT

their upbringing.

Breaking Generational Cycles

Generational financial struggles are often rooted in a lack of access to education and resources. Breaking this cycle requires intentional effort:

1. **Empower Yourself First:**
   - Before you can teach others, you must feel confident in your own financial knowledge and habits.
2. **Build Wealth Strategically:**
   - Use credit wisely, invest in opportunities that create long-term growth, and focus on assets that can be passed down.
3. **Share What You've Learned:**
   - Your journey—mistakes and successes alike—can inspire others in your family and community to take control of their finances.

Each step you take toward financial independence creates a ripple effect, showing those around you that change is possible and achievable.

The Bigger Picture: Credit, Wealth, and Community Impact

When you manage your credit and finances effectively, you're not just helping yourself—you're creating a foundation for future generations and contributing to your community. Here's how:

- **Creating Opportunities:** Good credit allows you to access resources that can uplift your family and community, like starting a business or providing affordable housing.
- **Building Wealth:** Wealth isn't just about money—it's about security, options, and the ability to give back. Strong financial habits enable you to accumulate and pass down assets that benefit others.
- **Inspiring Others:** Your success can motivate those around you to believe that financial freedom is within their reach.

Leaving a Legacy

Building a legacy isn't just about leaving money—it's about leaving knowledge, values, and opportunities. Here's how you can start:

1. **Pass on Financial Literacy:** Equip your children and community with the knowledge to make informed financial decisions.
2. **Invest in People and Projects:** Support initiatives that align with your values and create lasting change.
3. **Plan for the Future:** Use tools like wills, trusts, and life insurance to ensure your assets are distributed according to your wishes.

Your legacy is the impact you leave behind—on your family, your community, and the world.

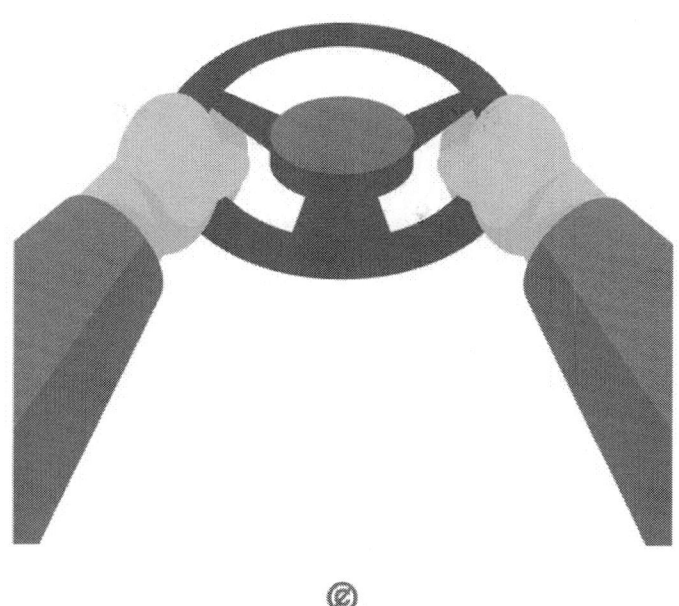

Key Takeaway

When you take control of your credit and finances, you're not just changing your life—you're changing the lives of those who come after you. By teaching financial literacy, breaking generational cycles, and contributing to your community, you can create a legacy of empowerment, opportunity, and lasting change.

CONCLUSION: CONFIDENCE OVER QUICK FIXES

Why Fixing Isn't the Answer

Throughout this journey, we've uncovered a fundamental truth: fixing your credit might seem like the easiest solution, but it's not the most effective one. Quick fixes offer temporary relief, but they don't address the habits, knowledge, and mindset needed for lasting change.

True confidence comes from understanding your credit, building good financial habits, and using credit as a tool to achieve your goals. It's about more than just raising a score—it's about transforming your relationship with money and taking control of your financial future.

TAKE OWNERSHIP OF YOUR JOURNEY

You've read about shifting your mindset, breaking free from systemic traps, building sustainable credit habits, and even leaving a legacy. Now it's your turn to take what you've learned and apply it to your life.

This isn't about perfection. It's about progress. It's about making intentional choices that align with your goals and moving forward, one step at a time. You don't need to have everything figured out today. You just need to start.

ONE SMALL STEP TODAY

The path to credit confidence begins with one small action. Maybe that's checking your credit report for the first time. Maybe it's setting up a budget or disputing an error on your report. Whatever your first step is, take it today.

Write down your goals. Define your why. Remind yourself of the life you're working toward and the legacy you want to leave behind. With every action, no matter how small, you're building a foundation for something bigger—something lasting.

You've Got This

Remember, your credit is a tool, not a measure of your worth. You are capable of learning, growing, and creating a financial future that serves you and your dreams. You're not alone on this journey, and every step you take brings you closer to the confidence, freedom, and opportunities you deserve.

The time to act is now. You've taken the first step by learning—now go build the financial life you've always envisioned.

Call-to-Action:

Start your journey today by doing one thing that moves you closer to your goals. Check your report, make a plan, or simply write down your "why." And if you need support, reach out—I'm here to help you every step of the way.

Final Section: Ready to Take the Next Step?

You've made it this far, and I hope you're feeling more confident about your financial journey. We've covered the importance of understanding credit, building good habits, and aligning your financial goals with your "why." But let's face it—credit repair is often one of the most intimidating parts of the process.

If you're ready to address those negative items on your credit report but don't know where to start, I want to introduce you to a tool that can help: **Dispute Beast**.

Dispute Beast

What Is Dispute Beast?

Dispute Beast is an AI-powered system designed to make the process of challenging inaccuracies on your credit report simple, effective, and stress-free. Whether you're dealing with outdated information, errors, or collections, Dispute Beast gives you the guidance and resources you need to tackle them head-on.

Dispute Beast

Why Choose Dispute Beast?

- **Ease of Use:** Designed to be simple and user-friendly, even for those new to credit repair.
- **Comprehensive Support:** You're never alone in the process.
  - Access our supportive **Facebook community**, where members share wins, tips, and encouragement.
  - Browse our in-depth **FAQs** to find answers to common questions.
  - Follow step-by-step **video guides** to make the process clear and manageable.
  - Need extra help? Reach out for **live support** from our team when you need personalized assistance.
- **Efficiency:** Save time and energy by letting Dispute Beast handle the heavy lifting of challenging inaccuracies.
- **Empowerment:** Take control of your credit with tools and resources that give you confidence in every step of the process.

TAKE THE FIRST STEP TODAY

If you're ready to start removing those negative items and continue building the financial future you deserve, visit disputebeast.com/durantent/ to learn more about Dispute Beast.

Remember, rebuilding your credit isn't about shortcuts—it's about making informed, intentional decisions every step of the way. Dispute Beast is here to support you on your journey.

Made in the USA
Middletown, DE
22 February 2025